The Creative Caregiver Presents...

Walk & Roll

Easy Sewing Projects to Assist Those with Special Mobility Needs

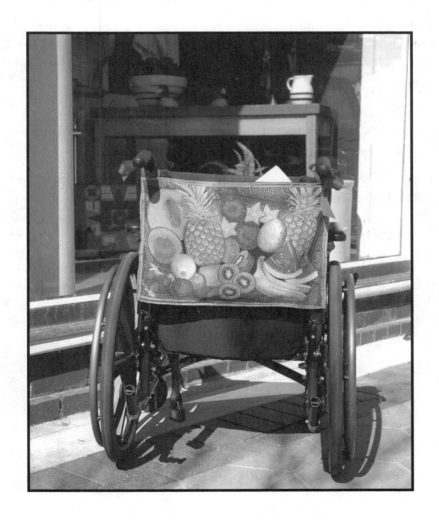

Lynn Lancaster Gorges

Published by Creative Caregiver

www.creativecaregiver.com
lynngorges@creativecaregiver.com
3910 Highway 70 East
New Bern, NC 28560
Fax 252-637-1862

ISBN: 1-4243-2186-7

ISBN-13: 978-1-4243-2186-5

LCCN 2007901464
ISBN 978-1-4243-2186-5

Dedication

My mother, Eva Pate Lancaster, inspired me to write this book, as well as my late father, Harold W. Lancaster, and late in-laws, Bill and Avis Gorges. Being an integral part of the "support team" our families formed for them as they required special care taught me new lessons on a daily basis. The needs of special people in my life – my friend Juanita Willis, my neighbors Tom Hott and Linda Clements, and my cousins Jodi Brookhart and Carly Cooper – have also contributed to my desire to help my loved ones.

Each of these very special people have faced extremely different challenges yet have shared so many similar ones as well. Over time, I have learned more and more from each unique experience.

Most of all, I dedicate this book to the loving grace of God. I feel strongly that God led me to fulfill this project so that others could reach out as caregivers.

Acknowledgements

My dear husband, William, and our precious children, Chris, Mark, and Nora, have put up with me while I sewed into the wee hours of the morning and endlessly cluttered our house with kitchen linens and mobility aids. Chris expertly rendered the line drawings, and William and Chris shared their wonderful editing skills to assist with this project as it neared the end. Their love for me, and faith in my mission, have been a constant source of strength.

My sister and best friend, Nan L. Davis, has been a major driving force the entire time I have worked on this project. She, too, saw it as a wonderful tribute to our mother. My brother and sister-in-law, Martin and Alice Lancaster, along with Nan, have been unbelievable caregivers for our mother. They have given Mama the very best of love and care on a daily basis for the past few years. Jim, my brother-in-law, and my husband, William, have cared for our homes and children many times when Nan and I have had to be away for endless trips to physicians, therapists and being with Mama for daily care at her home and in many facilities. Our children have supported us with love and patience. Uncle Hugh and Aunt Doris have cheered us on in all of our efforts to do the best we could for Mama. What an unbelievable circle of caring we have for Mama/Nana. Our "sandwich generation" family is a treasure!

Peggy Monterio, Shelby Bergland, Pepper Cory, Teresa Woock, Gaye Ingram, Pat Turlington, Rebecca Cline, and Emily Motley were there with me from the beginning to the end. They helped in any and every way possible, from sewing, to drawing, to finding artists, but mostly by brainstorming ideas with me. Peggy Monterio monogrammed the "leopard skin bag" for the book and did a super job. Daryl Johnson and Michael Holland at "Help at Home" were also wonderful, letting me use their equipment to "try things on" and offering me words of encouragement.

Many other dear friends too numerous to list have also been inspirational and kept me going. Often I would get off track and one of them would inquire about the progress of the book with great enthusiasm and convince me to get going again.

Cheryl Jukich was a tremendous help by assuring me early on that the dream of a book could become a reality. She gave me a great deal of good advice that headed me in the right direction.

Yvonne Gray (themousetamer.com) was with me all the way. She did a wonderful job with all of the photography, and her constant guidance and work on the layout was phenomenal. Yvonne also dealt with many roles as a caregiver during the process, as did I. Much of our work revolved around caregiving so we learned to "hurry up and wait" with much patience. We knew that our roles as caregivers took precedence.

Contents

Photos

(Photos shown left to right clockwise.)

Front Page – Seated Walker Coverup #2.

Back Page – Patetown Bag, Wheelchair Cover Up with pocket and pillow, Seated Walker Cover Up #1, Scooter Cover Up.

Red Page – Seated Walker Cover Up #1; Patetown bag; Red, White & Blue Wheelchair Cover Up; Wheelchair Cover Up (Sailboat variation).

Yellow Page – Atlantic bag, Greenville Bag, Goldsboro Bag, Wilson Bag.

Green Page – Wilmington Bag, Brimmed Hat Bag, Goldsboro Bags.

Blue Page – Wilmington Bag, New Bern Bag, Marine Patch Bag, License Plate Bag.

Photographs and book and cover layout by Yvonne Gray of Merritt, NC, (www.themousetamer.com).

W. Christopher Gorges provided the illustrations and editing.

Introduction

In 1991, at the age of 67 my mother suffered a severe stroke. Immediately, I began sewing aprons and clothing adaptations for her to accommodate the ensuing changes in her life. I enjoyed making Mama's daily life a little more pleasant and upbeat with pretty aprons. Modifying her clothing to make routine tasks easier for her seemed to be the least I could do to help. As the years passed, I also began to make things for relatives and friends who used walkers and wheelchairs.

In 2001, I made a bag for my mother's wheelchair using two inexpensive placemats. When she first saw the bag, she exclaimed, "Pretty!" This wouldn't be a ground-breaking revelation, except for the fact that in 2001, my mother was able to speak only once in a great while, and when she did, it was usually when she felt very strongly about something. So, with that one exclamation, I knew that the bag had truly struck a chord with her, and I felt that I may have hit on something even bigger.

The experience with that initial bag, now the pattern for the "Patetown Bag," led me to an important realization. Lots of pretty, inexpensive, and helpful items can be made from simple kitchen/table linens that are available to everyone, whether we live in rural areas or a big cities! Hence, the concept of turning kitchen linens into accessories and comfort items for the elderly and the disabled was born.

My mother was a wonderful volunteer in her church, the Extension Homemakers, and she was a charter member of the Reach to Recovery Group in our hometown of Goldsboro/Patetown, North Carolina. Mama wasn't a great seamstress, but she did love helping me with my sewing projects. I know she would have loved these items because she could have made or helped make these items for others in her community. Mama is still in a nursing home, so I am continuing to sew for her and her nursing home family.

My mother-in-law loved to sew and was a wonderful quilter. She would have loved the simplicity of these items and would have loved making them for her loved ones. Toward the end of her life, she spent a great deal of time in a wheelchair and was able to benefit from some of the items I created for her.

Sewing for loved ones made me realize that I needed to share this knowledge with others. Our parents would be pleased to know that the difficult times turned into a positive experience to help make life a little better for others. None of these items will ever cure cancer or prevent a stroke, but the items *can* make a cold and sterile piece of equipment more personal and functional – and certainly much more attractive. Most of all, it is my most sincere and deepest desire that the bags and covers will form a circle of love between the person who sews the item and the person who receives it. Showing love and creating smiles is what this book is all about!

Some Caregiver Statistics

- 52 million informal and family caregivers provide care to someone aged 20+ who is ill or disabled.
- 29.2 million family caregivers provide personal assistance to adults (aged 18+) with a disability or chronic illness.
- 34 million adults (16% of population) provide care to adults 50+ years.

  – See www.caregiver.org for more statistics

General Information

Kitchen & Table Linens

Kitchen and table linens work great for all of these projects. What an easy way to sew! There are no yardage measurements to work out and no patterns to cut out and pin.

You can go to a department store, discount store, outlet, or specialty shop to buy kitchen or table linens. The designs are fabulous! It's sometimes quite difficult not to buy several styles, since you can shop for linens that are perfect for all seasons and holidays, whether formal or casual. Most importantly, you can buy for your recipients' special interests and talents.

There are some important things to consider when buying the linens:

1. Not all linens are standard, so measure them and make sure to read their attached laundering directions.
2. If the item is to be used in a nursing home, trim should be minimal since nursing facility laundering can often be extremely harsh to fabrics. Laundry done at home is much easier on embellishments.

Make sure to tag your item with laundering instructions if it is going to be a gift – you certainly don't want the item ruined when being cleaned.

Basic Measurements for Kitchen or Table Linens

Remember that not all placemats, napkins, and kitchen towels are created equal! The basic measurements that most manufacturers use are given below. If you have a certain chair or walker in mind, make sure you measure it first for specifics. Then, when you're out shopping, always take along a tape measure.

If you can't find the kitchen/table linens that fit the "subject matter" you want for the recipient, purchase fabric by the yard. Patterns for making placemats are easily located in many bookstores and in your local library. Use your imagination to adapt. You can even quilt the fabric if you have those skills. The possibilities are endless!

Kitchen Linen Standard Measurements

- Placemats - 12" X 18", 13" X 19"
- 14" X 20" (oversized)
- Napkins - 18" X 18", 20" X 20"
- Kitchen Towels – 16" X 24", 16" X 28", 18" X 28", 20" X 28"

Metric Conversions

For those who use metric measurements, rather than standard, this is the basic way to convert measurements. The same method applies to lengths of ribbon, trim, Velcro™, sewing seams and other measurements given in the pattern instructions. Use this method if using yardage rather than store bought linens.

- Do the math -

1 inch = 25.4 mm = 2.54 cm

Here is an example of how to adapt a standard placemat to cloth yardage.

12" X 18" placemat =30.48 cm X 45.72 cm placemat

(12 X 2.54) = 30.48 cm (18 X 2.54) = 45.72 cm

To Convert	Into	Multiply by
centimeters	inches	.394
	feet	.0328
meters	centimeters	100
	inches	39.37
inches	centimeters	2.54
	feet	.0833
	meters	.0254
	yards	.0278

Sewing Information

Be sure to follow your sewing machine guidelines when sewing several layers of fabric in order to prevent damage to your machine. Be careful not to overtax your machine.

Seam allowances are roughly 1/2 inch (12.7 mm or 1.27 cm)

- Tie and cut threads after finishing a seam
- Press all seams as you sew
- Press the finished project
- Measure twice. Cut once.

NOTE: Read ALL instructions carefully before purchasing materials, cutting, or stitching in order to ensure final product quality.

Acronyms used throughout the book:

- RST: Right Sides Together
- WST: Wrong Sides Together
- RSO: Right Side Out
- WSO: Wrong Side Out

Basic Laundry Information

Most linens are 100% cotton so read and follow recommended washing instructions

Use Scotch Guard™ on any item you are concerned about getting dirty. Frequent washing is not necessary for most items due to the nature of their use. However, remember that most of the items presented in this book will need to be hand laundered and ironed after extended periods of use.

Close Velcro™ strips so that the "teeth" do not attach themselves to other items of clothing when washing or drying. Refer to the section on Kitchen and Table Linens for more information.

Information About All Mobility Aids

This entire book is focused on wheelchairs, walkers, seated walkers (often called Rollators™), electric scooters and other mobility aids. Please remember that it was impossible to try the patterns on ALL models. Many companies manufacture assorted mobility aids, so wide variations in size and design exist on the market. For example, wheelchair arms attach in many different ways, the width of the arm rests vary, and seats come in all sizes and shapes.

It's my hope that you will find several patterns that you can adapt to your particular needs and resources. If a particular item you want to make needs to fit snuggly or needs to fit around tubular bars, please make sure you measure first. These patterns are super simple. With slight modifications, they will work for nearly all models.

Bag Embellishments

Many bags, especially the Patetown bag, offer you a clean palette to accent a person's special interests. Sew on patches, hats and banners, iron on appliqué squares, or samples of handiwork such as crocheted doilies. Go up in the attic to find some old mementoes from hobbies, sports, or vacations. Get out those old neckties, special laces, scarves, quilt squares, belt buckles, and costume jewelry. Old sewing baskets and jewelry boxes might hold some extra special treasures for embellishing. Your hunt might turn up some great conversation pieces!

CAUTION: Important !

Here are some important things you should consider before you apply a trim:

- How will the item be laundered, and by whom? Remember, nursing facilities use extremely hot water for laundering and generally do not iron items. Ribbon could possibly end up shrinking or fading and buttons could break or fall off.

- Who will be using the bag? Is there a possibility that parts of the bag may lead to choking and/or injury? Make sure you know the limitations and risks you might face with the recipient. Alzheimer's patients and children should have all attached items sewn on very securely with buttonhole thread or dental floss. Always be safety-conscious when selecting trim and decorations for your creations.

Decorative Trim

Selecting decorative trim can be a great deal of fun. Look at crafts books and sewing books for a multitude of ideas. There are many fun ideas waiting to be adapted to your needs. The trims often put the pizzazz in a project!

Ribbon, Binding, Rickrack & Fringe

- Stitch trim in rows or around the top
- Gather ribbon as a ruffle
- Pleat ribbon and stitch in place
- Tie bows and then safety pin on the bag or tack stitch in the center
- Use ribbon as the holders/hangers
- Stitch as a trim around the top of the bag
- Use sequins or fake fur for an accent

Buttons

- Glue them or stitch them on in a design or at random
- Cover buttons in a contrasting fabric
- Use as closures with a looped piece of elastic

Monograms & Appliques

- Initials (professionally stitched lettering or purchased adhesive letters)
- Names
- Flowers, soccer balls, fish, etc.

Don't forget decorative machine stitching and quilting!

Photo Pocket

You can adorn any of these bags with one or a few favorite photographs. Get out some old photo albums and have a blast picking out photos that your loved one would like to show off and talk about with his or her friends. Selecting just one might be too difficult so why not put on two or three pockets? Don't forget to change the photos every few weeks. Coordinating them with the holidays can be an added bonus. Highlighting postcards from vacations or family trips work well also.

MATERIALS & NOTIONS

Kitchen linens to suit bag of choice
Photo pocket or clear plastic sheeting
Photos
Optional - Trim at least 24 inches long
(rick rack, ribbon, braid, etc.)
Glue

---

1.   Select the type of bag you will be putting the photo pocket on. Think of the person's mobility equipment and decide how to highlight the photo.

2.   Select the linen item that will be the front of the bag. Lay the photo on the kitchen linen item. Two or 3 photos on the front of the bag might be perfect for a larger bag.

3. Use the original photo or take it to a local store to alter the size or to crop it.

4. Cut a plastic rectangle 6 inches X 4 inches or use a photo album pocket. (**In order to stitch over the plastic, you need to place a piece of tissue paper over the plastic. This prevents sticking.)

5. If using trim, glue it onto the edges or stitch/baste in place. Let glue dry.

6. Place the pocket on the front of the kitchen linen. Pin in the corners. (Make sure the opening for the photo is on the side or on the top.)

7. Topstitch in place.

8. Finish bag according to the instructions given. Attach a tied bow or a sprig of holly with fabric glue if you like.

Other Pocket Options

Purchased items such as pencil bags, makeup bags, and other small zippered pouches are quite helpful and attractive.

1. Stitch just the corners, across the top, or down the side seams and along the bottom.

2. *Freezer style Zip Lock™ bags* are easy to sew onto bags that won't be used often or when only lightweight items are carried often.

3. Stitch along the top back portion or down the sides.

4. Place tissue paper on top so that it will feed better when stitching.

A cloth napkin cut in half is perfect if you decide you would like a matching pocket with a zipper inside. For those who are already familiar with sewing in zippers, it's a breeze.

1. Turn under the raw edge, and press with an iron.

2. Pin the pocket inside or on the outside of the bag.

3. Stitch around the sides and bottom.

Bag Handles & Hangers

The Different Types

Using different kinds of handles/hangers on a bag is a terrific way to make it unique. I've suggested ones that seem to work best on specific bags. But don't just do it my way – use these techniques to make a bag look masculine or feminine!

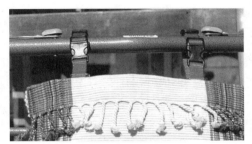

Dog collar

Ribbon ties

Velcro

D-ring

STITCHING NOTE: Stitch back and forth several rows of stitching to make sure that the loop will be secure when the bag is holding items, or stitch in a square or "X" pattern.

Dog Collar

Purchase two (2) inexpensive adjustable nylon dog collars at your local dollar or bargain store (collar measurements should be 1-inch wide, fitting a 16- to 22-inch neck). The selection of bright colors is fantastic!

NOTE: This is much less expensive than purchasing the webbing, slides, and the pinch-type closures.

1. Open the collar and lay it flat. Adjust it almost to its full length.

2. Pin the collar in place on the bag to get a feel for how long you want the handle to be. The measurements given below are for a length I like, but you can adjust them to your own needs.

3. Cut the collar on the female closure side 1 to 2 inches below the D-ring (Note: D-ring works well as a key chain holder).

4. Put glue or Fray Check™ on the cut edge. Allow to dry.

5. Adjust the long side with the sliding adjuster so that the length of that side is 4 inches (double thickness) from the closure adjuster and the collar adjuster. There should be a tail below the adjuster several inches long.

6. Cut it so you have only a 1-inch tail below the adjuster. Finish that edge with glue/Fray Check™. (You now have made it so that the length of the holders can be adjusted several inches.)

7. If you plan to have a folded-over cuff, you need to do that now to determine where the collar should be stitched. Place pins where the holders should be stitched. Flip the cuff back up.

8. Pin the 4 collar pieces about 2 or 3 inches in from the side seams on the inside of the bag. (If you put them on the corners, the bag will gape open.)

9. Stitch in a box pattern with a zigzag stitch.

10. Turn down cuff.

Velcro™ (1 side loop/1 side hook)

(or any brand of hook and loop fastener)

The Patetown and Goldsboro Bags

1. Cut two hook pieces and two loop pieces of Velcro™, all 4 inches long

2. Stitch sides of folded placemat, following pattern for the Patetown and Goldsboro bags.

3. Lay loop piece on top of hook piece, both facing up (so they don't attach to each other). Repeat for other two pieces.

4. Place pieces of Velcro™ in the top corners of bag so they are sandwiched on the bag's inside.

5. Pin so 3 inches of Velcro™ are above the bag's edge.

6. Stitch straps in place securely.

7. Fold the hook piece on top of the loop piece once you have wrapped it around the tubular rail of the walker or the arm of wheelchair.

Four Corner Hanger

1. Stitch the sides of the bag together.

2. Stitch the corners following the *Wilmington Bag* instructions. (Illustration #1)

3. Decide if you want a turned-down edge on the top of the bag.

4. Position the Velcro, ribbons or cut dog collars along the top edges an inch or two from the side seams.

5. Pin in place. (If using Velcro™ make sure that it is placed so that it will attach when folded over a tubular rail.)

6. Stitch securely.

One-Wrap Velcro™

This type of Velcro™ has loops on one side and hooks on the other. You can purchase it in hardware or office supply stores. It is often used as a cable tie.

1. Determine the length needed to wrap around the arm or rail. Make sure you allow at least 2 inches of overlap.
2. Cut two pieces (one for each corner).
3. Fold both pieces in half to find their centers. Pin at centers.
4. Sandwich Velcro™ pieces in between the placemats at upper corners.
5. Stitch all layers together securely.

Snag-Free Velcro with a Ring

1. Purchase two 1-inch plastic rings or two 1-inch D-rings
2. Cut two 8-inch long pieces of Snag Free Velcro™
3. Loop the Velcro™ thru the ring with the hook sides facing each other about 1 inch. This will leave a 7-inch tail.
4. Pin the Velcro™/ring portion on the back corners of the bag so that the 7-inch tail is lying along the back with the hook side facing down. The ring will be visible over top edge.
5. Stitch back and forth over the folded Velcro™.

NOTE: The Velcro™ will now loop over an armrest or rail and pass through the ring. Fold the Velcro™ back over itself in order to adjust to the arm or rail.

Ribbon

When using ribbon handles, you can easily tie bows to secure the bag to your wheelchair or walker of choice!

NOTE: When sewing ribbon on the Envelope Bag, stitch the folded-over ribbon to the outside of the back of the bag at the top corners. Fold the top flap up to pin. Stitch.

Folded Loop Ribbon

This works well on walker bags. Place the loops over 2 decorative shower hooks on the top bar of the walker.

1. Cut 2 pieces of 1-inch wide ribbon 5 inches long
2. Fold the ribbon so it forms a loop with the front side of the ribbon facing out.
3. Pin cut ends together into upper corners between the layers of placemat.
4. Stitch securely.
5. Hang two shower hooks on walker and place folded ribbon loops over them.

Important Closure Notes!

Bags with stitched corners often need closures in the center.

Some options:

1. Stitch a button on the front side and sew a loop on the back.
2. Stitch small dots or squares of Velcro™ on the inside center top of the bag.
3. Attach a magnetic closure following manufacturer's directions.

My Notes

Seated Walker Cover-up

The Patetown Bag

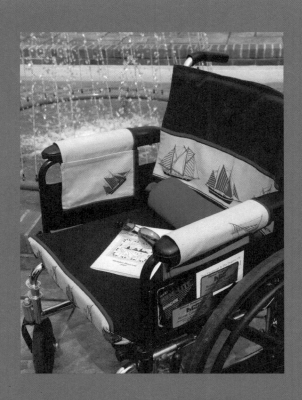

Sailboat Wheelchair Cover-up

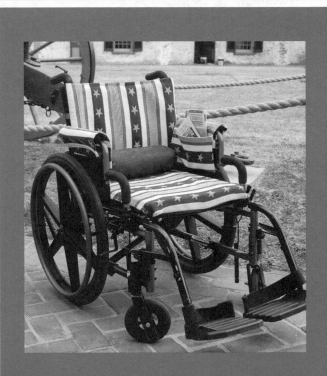

Wheelchair Cover-up

The Wilmington Bag

The New Bern Bag

The License Plate Bag

The Marine Patch Bag

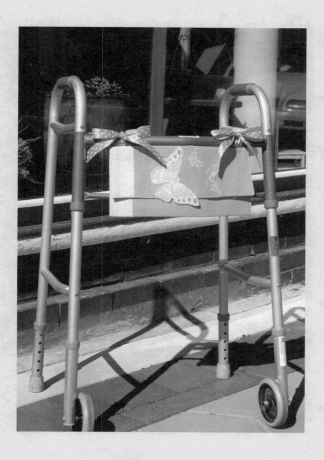

The Atlantic Bag

The Greenville Bag

The Wilson Bag

The Goldsboro Bag

The Wilmington Bag

The Brimmed Cap Bag

The Goldsboro Bag

Seated Walker Cover-ups

The seated walkers, often called Rollators™, are all the rage! It gives folks a walker with brakes and the added bonus of a seat and a basket. There are lots of colors and several different configurations. However, it can get a bit confusing in a health care facility to decide to whom the chairs belongs. For the "at home users" it is nice to blend their walker with their décor.

Give that great little buggy a personality to match its driver. With so many wonderful fabrics available, I just couldn't stop making these so there are 3 different patterns for making the covers. Let's get rolling!

Seat Cover #2

(Shown on front cover)

NOTE: The model used for this book has the basket under the padded seat. Others have the basket out in the front. Not all have padded seats. Make sure you know these facts before you begin to sew.

On the seats I recommend that you use smooth cotton kitchen towels, not the loopy terry cloth variety. Those terry cloth loops are just too easy to pick and pull with frequent use and laundering. Save the terry cloth ones for the bags that won't be used quite as much.

Seated Walker Cover-up #1

Seat Cover #1

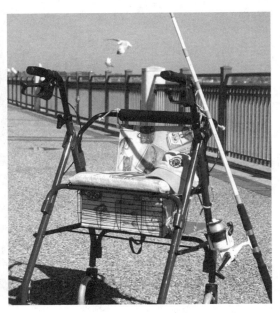

MATERIALS & NOTIONS

(Placemat version – very easy)
Thread
1 Placemat
36 inches of 1-inch wide Elastic
Optional edge trim if your seat is a little wider

---

1. Place placemat on seat and decide if you want to put trim on the long edge of the placemat to cover the edge of the cushion.

2. If you are using trim, cut the trim the same length as the longest side of the placemat, adding an inch at each end to turn under (to avoid a raw edge). Either sew it on the front only or on both of the long edges.

3.   Cut elastic into three 12-inch long pieces.

4.   Lay placemat face down. Find center of the short sides and pin a piece of elastic onto the center of the right-side edge. Elastic should lie to the side horizontally, not vertical. See Illustration.

5.   Pin second piece of elastic about 1 inch below top right corner.

6.   Pin third piece of elastic 1 inch above bottom right corner.

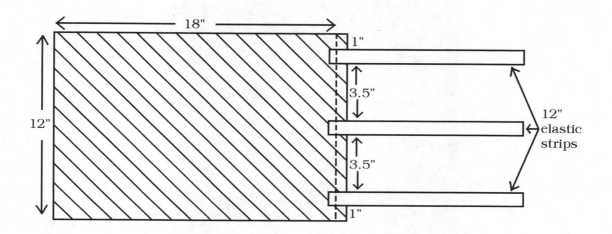

7.   Pin loose ends of elastic to corresponding positions on left side of placemat.

8.   Zigzag stitch all three pieces of elastic on both sides.

9.   Turn right side out and slide the cover onto the seat.

*** Hint: Just in case the seat cover slides around a little, buy some of the rug or shelf lining gripping material. There are also placemats made of this material so you can buy a small piece and place it between the cover and the cushion.

Backrest Bar Bag #1

Goldsboro Bag

The Backrest Bar Bag is a simple bag that you can easily hang on the back bar rest of a Rollator™ walker or anywhere else you find fitting.

MATERIALS & NOTIONS

1 Placemat
24 inches of ribbon/cord/rope, etc. for hangers
Thread

Fishing Fabric

1. Fold placemat in half with WST.
2. Pin sides.
3. Stitch
4. Attach hanger/handles of choice.

Red Print Fabric

1.   Fold in half.

2.   Fold the front down 3 inches to form a cuff in the front. Stitch down sides.

3.   Attach holders/handles of choice at the top corners.

4.   Pin on at a slight angle if you want to use this on a Rollator® Backrest Bar. This positions the ribbons to go on either side of the rubber grip.

Basket Liner #1

MATERIALS & NOTIONS

Thread
1 Placemat
24 inches ribbon/rope, etc.

Special Notes: The Fishing Fabric example uses jute twine as ties. The Red print fabric example has ribbon ties. Use a placemat with 2 pretty sides if possible!

1.   Measure the bottom of the basket. The following instructions are given for a basket that is 6 inches across the bottom. If your basket is different, simply adjust steps and measurements accordingly.

2.   Find the center of the placemat along the long edge. Mark with a pin.

3.   If the basket is 6 inches across the bottom, put a pin at 3" on each side of the center pin. Do this on both sides.

4.   Remove center pin. Tri-fold into the center (as if folding a letter to put into an envelope) along the other pin marks. When folding and pressing, remember the attractive side will face out on the sides of the basket.

5.   Press.

6.   Stitch along press lines on the right side. This gives definition to the liner.

7.   Cut ribbon into four 6-inch pieces. Cut ends on a slant for decorative touch.

8.   Fold ribbons in half and pin in each of the four corners of the placemat.

9.   Stitch on ribbons.

10.   Place inside basket with wrong side facing up and pretty sides facing out.

11.   Tie ribbons to hold in place.

Transporting a Seated Walker

Transporting a seated walker is often frustrating as it will unfold and be difficult to handle. To tackle this problem purchase LARGE Velcro™ Straps from your hardware store. Fold up the walker and then wrap the Velcro™ straps around the support bars in front and behind the folded seat. No more problems with the walker unfolding as you are trying to lift it into or out of your car!

Seated Walker Cover-up #2

Seat Cover #2

Made with Kitchen Towels

This cover will probably become a constant favorite. It can be adapted to a multitude of fabrics. The seat cover might be a little tricky at first but once you get the idea, it will zip right along.

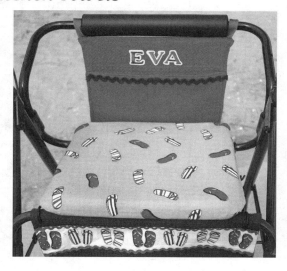

MATERIALS & NOTIONS

Thread
1 Smooth Surface Kitchen Towel (26 inches x 17 inches)
12-inch piece of Elastic (1/4-inch wide)

Place towel on seat. Determine orientation of design in relation to seat. Remember that this will slide onto the fold-up seat like a pillowcase. The folded edge will be at the front of the seat.

READ THIS BEFORE PROCEEDING

1.   You might have to cut the towel in order to orient the design properly. (For example, you wouldn't want a cat design to be upside down when you look at it while holding the handlebars.)

2.   If the design is oriented properly, skip steps 3–8 and move ahead to *Sewing Instructions*.

3.   If you need to cut your towel in order to orient the designs correctly, DO NOT CUT IT IN HALF! Place towel on seat. Pin it to determine how it will fit when sewn. The top portion of the seat cover should be 4 inches longer than the other part to make sure it will fold over the back of the cushion. Pin along the cutting line.

4.   Fold, press, and THEN cut along the fold.

5.   Placing RST, pin top of newly cut edge of shorter fabric section to bottom of already-hemmed edge of longer fabric section. Stitch sections together with the raw edge next to the hemmed edge.

6.   For a decorative edge, stitch ribbon on top of new seam.

7.   Turn under other raw edge at the end twice. Pin. Topstitch.

8.   Proceed to the sewing instructions.

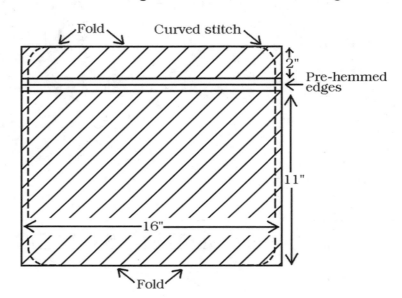

Sewing instructions

1.   Fold towel RST so that the sides are 11 inches with a 4-inch single thickness at the top. Fold 4-inch section RST to form a 2-inch side. (See illustration above.)

2.   Pin and stitch sides.

3.   Draw a curve on the wrong side of the corners with a highlighter pen. Use a soda or similar can to get a good curve.

4.   Stitch along curved lines.

5. Slide cover onto seat cushion. Trim off excess fabric inside after you're sure it fits correctly.

6. Turn right side out. Press.

7. Slide onto the seat like a pillowcase.

Note: If you have a thicker cushion and want to make a corner fit better, follow Wilmington Bag illustration #2.

Decorative Skirt & Basket Liner #2

MATERIALS & NOTIONS

1 Decorative bordered Kitchen Towel
1 16-inch strip of hook & loop Velcro™
1 12-inch strip of Ribbon

Kitchen towels often have great decorative borders. Borders can become adorable skirts for seated walkers.

Skirt

1. Hang a decorative bordered towel over the front bar that the seat folds down and rests on.

2. Decide how much fabric you want as an overhang for the specific walker.

3. Allow 2 additional inches (For example, if you want 6 inches to overhang, measure 8 inches of towel).

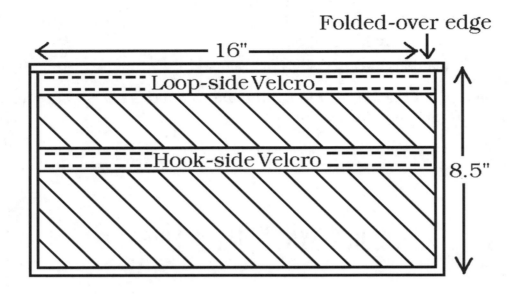

4. Measure and cut fabric. (See illustration above.)

5. Lay the large portion aside to use for "Basket Liner #2".

6. Turn under the raw edge 1/2 inch. Press.

7. Place one 16-inch strip of Velcro™ on the wrong side on top of turned-over raw edge. Pin.

8. Pin other 16-inch strip of Velcro™ tape 3 inches parallel to first Velcro™ strip, also on the wrong side. Determine where the stitching will be on the front before you stitch. Make sure that it will look nice on the decorative side. Move second strip up or down as needed.

9. Stitch Velcro™ strips in place. Press and attach around walker bar.

24

Basket Liner #2

Use the remaining portion of above towel to make a liner for the walker's basket. Remember that not all kitchen towels are the same size, so be flexible.

1. Cut towel so dimensions are 14 inches by 17 inches.
2. Turn under the raw edge twice. Pin, press, and topstitch.
3. Cut four 3-inch pieces of ribbon.
4. Fold each ribbon so it forms a loop with the front side of the ribbon facing out. Pin two cut ends of ribbon together. Refer to the *Folded Loop Ribbon* instructions.
5. Pin a ribbon loop on the right side of each corner so they will fit on the corner basket hooks. Zigzag stitch or turn under the raw edges of the ribbons and then stitch.

NOTE: The liner will cover the longest sides of the basket. The ends will be open.

Backrest Bar Bag #2

Eva Bag

With several small pockets and a large pocket to carry magazines or books, this bag is a big helper all day long whether on the beach or at home. It also offers a nice place above the smaller pockets to showcase someone's name or initials. I used the easy iron-on type letters to spell out my mother's name.

MATERIALS & NOTIONS

Kitchen towel
Masking tape
Two 3-inch pieces Velcro®
Thread
Fabric Glue
Optional - iron-on letters

---

1. Fold kitchen towel in half RST with short edges touching. (See illustration #1.)

2. Pin along that edge and stitch.

3. Trim off the bulky pre-hemmed edge. Turn RSO and press.

4. To determine where the center line will be for 2 small front pockets, place a 6-inch piece of masking tape up the center of the bottom along center line. (See illustration # 2.)

5. Stitch beside the edge of the tape for a straight line.

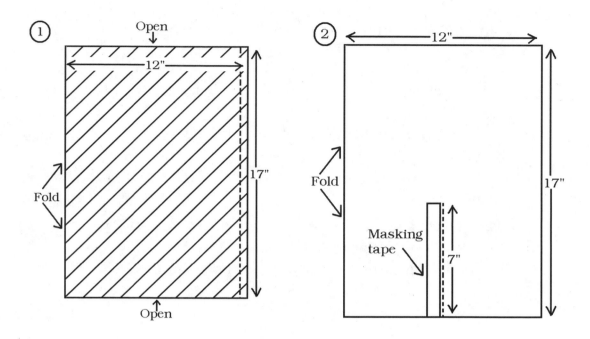

6. Fold bottom up at the point of the top of the 6-inch stitch. Press. Pin sides and stitch along edges. (See illustration #3.)

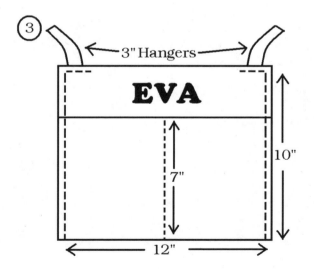

Now, look at the section on **Bag Handles/Hangers** *and decide which type you prefer. The "flip flop" example uses the Velcro™ hanger, but any of the hangers will work just fine.*

1. For the Velcro™ hanger cut four 5-inch Velcro™ strips (2 hook, 2 loop).
2. Pull apart and lay them so that the back of the hook piece is lying on top of the loop.
3. Pin them inside the corners top corners of the bag at a slight angle.
4. Stitch in place.
5. Using fabric glue, attach rickrack or other border of your choice to the edge of two small pockets.
6. Iron-on initials or names are a good choice for this bag.

BAG OPTION

In order to stabilize the bag more, you might want to attach the bottom corners of the bag to the side rails. Stitching ribbons or Velcro™ to the lower corners is an option. If you don't plan on the bag carrying very much weight, leave it as is.

Bogue Sound Bag

Variation on the Eva Bag

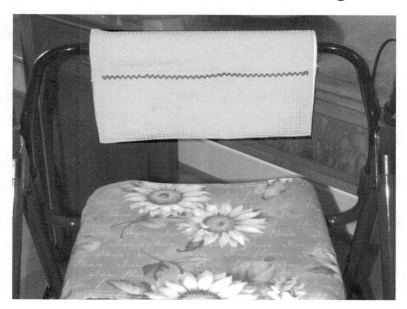

<u>Materials and Notions</u>

1 dish towel, which is the same on both sides
12 inches hook & loop Velcro™
Optional: Rick rack, ribbon, etc.
Thread

---

1.   Fold kitchen towel in half WST with short edges touching. Press. (Use illustration #1 for Eva Bag, but remember WST not RST.)

Note: If you want trim stitched along the edge, do it now. Pin the trim along the upper right side edge of half of the towel. Stitch in place.

2.   Pin along the longest open side. Stitch.

3.   To determine where the center line will be for the two small front pockets, place a 5-inch piece of masking tape up the center of the bottom along the center line. (Use illustration #2 for Eva Bag, but put the masking tape line at 5 inches, NOT 7 inches.)

4.   Turn up the 5-inch pockets and press along the bottom fold line. Mark or place pins on the sides to determine where the top of the pocket will be. (Don't sew the sides until both pieces of Velcro™ are stitched on the back.)

5.   Flip over with the pocket facing down on the work table.

6.   Pin the hook side of the Velcro™ to the top short edge opposite the folded pocket edge.

7.   Stitch around all sides of the Velcro.

8.   Take pins out of the pocket so the item is flat. Leave pins on the sides to mark the top of the pocket. Pin the second piece of Velcro™ on the back slightly below where the top of the pocket will be. This will ensure that the pocket will conceal the stitching.

9.   Stitch the Velcro strip around all edges.

10.   Turn over to the front side. Flip the lower edge up to form the pocket.

11.   Pin along the pocket sides. Stitch and press.

12.   Item is now completed. Attach it to the backrest bar by putting the Velcro together with the pockets facing the seat area.

Wheelchair Cover-up

Many folks seem to be customizing their cars these days, so it's only fitting to do some custom work on wheelchairs. This can be a novel way to turn a very functional piece of equipment into something that everyone around can admire and enjoy aesthetically!

You can purchase chair seat cushions to match placemat fabric or you can sew a cushion cover. Make sure you know all about the wheelchair cushion before deciding. Next, sew a covering for the back of the seat and the side arms. You might even "take it over the edge" with a cute little ruffle along the front of the seat. What a genteel touch!

It's especially nice to have a custom covered chair in nursing facilities, since wheelchairs often get mixed up because they are all so similar. When you're finished with it, your loved one's wheelchair will be transformed into a true declaration of personal taste! Get ready to do some wheelies!

NOTE: Special sewing notes for seat cover to ensure a proper fit

- Measure the cushion covers before you proceed with the project. Seats vary greatly depending on the size of the person who uses the chair.
- Seat cushions are often gel-filled or specially contoured foam to prevent pressure sores. Make sure the cover doesn't interfere with the function of the cushion. Better yet, check with the person's physical therapist.
- As a safety feature, seat cushions often have Velcro™ strips on the bottom that adhere to the seat of the chair to prevent sliding. Make sure that the cover doesn't interfere with this Velcro™.
- Consider laundering and hygiene issues when selecting the fabric, since seat covers should be laundered more than the other covers.
- You will find a few cushions that are small enough to cover with a placemat, but most of the time a cloth dinner napkin is best.

Make sure you measure the seat cushion before shopping for supplies in order to ensure a proper fit. A standard placemat is about 18" X 12". Your seat cushion may be larger than this.

If you really want to use placemat-type fabric, you can:

- Modify by purchasing a table runner.
- Extend the width of the placemat with another placemat.
- Extend the width with fabric from a matching/coordinating napkin.

Wheelchair Seat Cover

This simple cover works well on all of the wheelchair seats seen in the photographs. Maybe you should make several since the seat will get the most wear!

MATERIALS & NOTIONS

Thread
1 Cloth Napkin or a Table Runner
1 Seat Cushion (standard with chair or purchased)
Three 15-inch pieces of 1-inch wide elastic
or
Three 10-inch hook & loop Velcro™

Note: If you place a ruffle on the front, place the elastic/Velcro™ strips that go underneath the cushion on the sides rather than the front and back.

1. Lay cloth on seat to determine its design orientation (most napkins are square).

2. Cut elastic into three 15-inch pieces. Or, cut three 10-inch strips of 2-sided Velcro™.

3. Lay napkin face down. Find center of the side edge and pin a piece of elastic onto the center of the right-side edge. Elastic should lie to the side horizontally, not vertical. (See illustration on the next page.)

4. Pin second piece of elastic about 1 inch below top right corner.

5. Pin third piece of elastic 1 inch above bottom right corner.

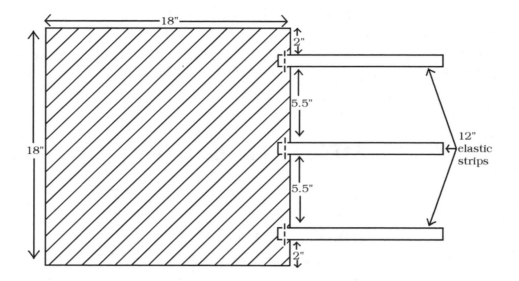

6.   Pin loose ends of elastic to corresponding positions on left side of napkin.

7.   Zigzag stitch all three pieces of elastic on both sides.
      Slide the cover onto the cushion.

8.   To add a skirt, go to the section "Ruffled Cushion Skirt".

A Simple Boxed Edge for Seat Cover

1.   Place the cover on the seat WSO.

2.   Fold the corners as you would if wrapping a present.

3.   Pin, and stitch along the folds.

Seat Back Cover With Pocket & Pillow

NOTE: Sew this section in two parts.

MATERIALS & NOTIONS

Thread
3 Placemats (4 if you decide to make a pillow for the back)
One 36-inch piece of 1-inch wide Ribbon
or
8 inches of hook & loop Velcro™
2 ounces of Polyester Craft Filling
(1/4 of an 8-ounce bag)

Part 1: Pocket Back

(The illustration for this pattern are on the next page.)

1. Fold one placemat in half horizontally. Press.
2. Position folded placemat on the right side of another placemat, aligned with bottom edge.
3. Pin and stitch sides and along bottom.
4. Measure 3 inches down from two upper corners. Mark with pins.
5. Cut 36-inch piece of ribbon into four equal pieces (Or cut four 3-inch long Velcro™ pieces. Velcro™ doesn't need turning under.
6. Fold under 1 inch of each ribbon. Press.
7. Pin folded-under ends of two of the ribbons at 3-inch marks. Stitch.

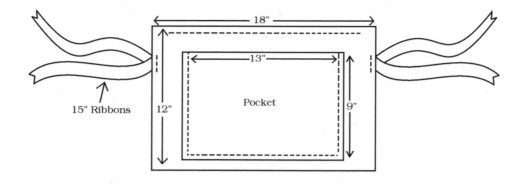

Seat Back Cover Illustration

Part 2: Pillow

Front of Seat Back With a Pillow

1. Place 2 placemats WST.
2. Measure 3 inches down on each side from two upper corners. Mark with pins.
3. Sandwich a ribbon or Velcro™ pieces at marks on each side 3 inches down from corners.
4. Stitch up the sides, across the top, and partially along the bottom, leaving a 4-inch opening.
5. Stuff filling in between placemats through the opening. (You be the judge of how full to stuff it.)
6. Pin opening closed.
7. Stitch.
8. Lay the back cover (placemat) on a table with the pocket facing down.
9. Lay the pillow back cover on top of it.
10. Pin along the top of the pocketed back and the other back.
11. Measuring 3 inches in from the top corners (along the top edge), pin the two pieces together.

12.	Stitch along the top, allowing the 3 inches on each side to remain unstitched to make room for wheelchair push handles.

13.	Place on chair back and secure with Velcro™ or ribbons.

Rolled Pillow

The Rolled Pillow is the perfect finishing touch for the Wheelchair Cover! It's also great way to provide some extra lower-back support.

MATERIALS & NOTIONS

1 Cloth Napkin (most napkins are 20 X 20 inches)
Two 20-inch pieces of ribbon
2 ounces of craft-type Polyester Filling

1.	Cut napkin so its dimensions are 13 inches by 20 inches.

2.	Lay napkin flat with right side down and turn up left and right pre-hemmed side seams 1 inch.

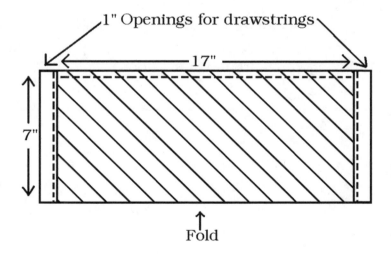

1" Openings for drawstrings

17"

7"

Fold

3. Press and pin.

4. Stitch along right and left edges to provide pockets for threading ribbon.

5. Fold the napkin lengthwise RST. Pin along the open edge.

6. Stitch edges together, leaving ½-inch seam allowance on each side for ribbon pockets.

7. Press seam and turn RSO.

8. Thread ribbons thru the pockets on each end.

9. Fill large empty space with polyester filling.

10. Draw ends closed and tie ribbons in bows.

Creative Uses for Everyday Items

1. Plastic cable ties work well to attach bags, bike horns, cup holders, an umbrella in a bag, etc.

2. Zippered school supply bags with grommet holes can fit on the rails using the plastic cable ties or Velcro™cable ties.

3. Small dog collars are perfect for holding a milk crate type storage cube in a wheelchair user's lap while shopping or moving items around in the house.

Arm Rest Cover

MATERIALS & NOTIONS

Thread
1 Placemat
1 Matching/coordinating Cloth Napkin
16 inches of 1-inch wide hook & loop Velcro™

NOTE: This pattern will only work if the arm of the wheelchair is open underneath it. If there is a post holding the arm in place you will have to use the "Snag Free Velcro/D-ring" method of securing the cover to the chair arm.

1. To make the two pockets fold napkin in half WST. Cut on fold.
2. Lay one piece aside. Fold one piece vertically. Pin raw edges.
3. Stitch raw edge side and turn RSO. Pocket should be no deeper than 6 or 7 inches.
4. Push out corners, press, and set aside.
5. Repeat steps 2, 3, and 4 with the second piece to make the second pocket.
6. Fold placemat in half RST. Cut on fold.
7. Turn cut edge under. Pin. Topstitch with a straight or zigzag stitch.
8. Position one pocket (half napkin) along the bottom edge of the arm cover (half placemat).
9. Place pins in placemat fabric to mark where you will be sewing on the pocket then lay pocket aside.
10. Repeat steps 7, 8, and 9 with the second half of the placemat and the second pocket.
11. Cut four 8-inch pieces Velcro™.
12. Flip over placemat with the pocket side facing down.
13. Pin one side of the Velcro™ along the top short edge of the back side.

14. Stitch on Velcro™.

15. Following the marker pins on the sides of the placemat, pin second piece of Velcro™ (Make sure it's the piece that will stick to the one you've already stitched in!) so it is slightly below the top edge of the pocket on the backside. This way the pocket will conceal the stitching.

16. Stitch on strips of Velcro™ securely.

17. Turn over to front side.

18. Pin pockets in place and stitch along the sides and bottom to form pockets.

19. Hang over each wheelchair and secure with Velcro™.

Ruffled Cushion Skirt

Many women love ruffled/frilly decorating. For those women this is the perfect "icing on the cake" for a wheelchair cover.

<u>MATERIALS & NOTIONS</u>

1 Cloth Napkin
1 Completed Seat Cover for Wheelchair (made from napkin)
Thread

---

1.   Measure and cut two 4-inch wide strips of fabric (It's best if you can use two pieces with one cut edge and one hemmed edge).

NOTE: Since you are cutting this napkin into two strips to stitch together, you need to make sure the pattern lines up properly along the center seam before cutting.

Measure <u>TWICE</u> and cut <u>ONCE</u>!

Refer to illustration before proceeding

2.   Pin two short ends together on hemmed edges.

3.   Stitch and press.

4.   Stitch a long gathering stitch along the top raw edge. Gather.

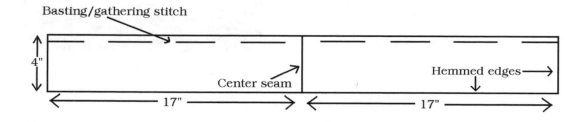

5.   Pin ruffle RST to the seat cover's front edge.

6.   Determine if you want the ruffle straight across or with an inch or two turning the corner. (It's a matter of personal preference, and depends on the cushion, chair, and fabric you use.)

7.   Press the ruffle so that it lays flat.

8.   Topstitch along the top edge.

Wheelchair Back Cover

Patriotic Fabric Variation

This design would make a great special gift for a veteran or soldier in a rehabilitation program. Loved ones and those involved with service projects for soldiers will find this style of cover especially useful.

MATERIALS & NOTIONS

Thread
2 Placemats
Two 2-inch pieces of hook & loop Velcro™

---

1. Place the two placemats WST.

2. Pin along the top edge. Stitch across the top but leave 3 inches open on each side.

3. Three inches down from top corners of bottom placemat, pin loop pieces of Velcro™ to side edges (on wrong side, not side with pattern), with about 1-1/2 inches hanging off to the side and loops facing down.

4. Three inches down from top corners of top placemat, pin hook pieces of Velcro™ to side edges (on wrong side, not side with pattern), with about 1-1/2 inches hanging off to the side with hooks facing down. (These positionings allow the user to secure the cover to the back of the wheelchair, preventing it from sliding.)

5. Stitch pieces of Velcro™ in place, slide over wheelchair back, and secure Velcro™ straps.

Patriotic Side Arm Bags

This variation on the **Side Arm Bag** complements the Patriotic Wheelchair Cover perfectly. Wheelchair users are able to have two pockets on each side for remote controls, telephone, wallet, a book, or any number of other small- to medium-sized objects. Velcro™, thread, and a napkin are the only items you need to get going on this project!

MATERIALS & NOTIONS

2 Large Cloth Napkins
Two 8-inch pieces of hook & loop Velcro™
Thread

---

1. Fold napkin in half WST and press along fold.
2. Pin along the open long side. Stitch.
3. Turn up one of the short open ends 5 or 6 inches to form a pocket. Press along fold. Mark or pin on the sides to determine where the top of the pocket will be. (Don't sew the sides until both pieces of Velcro™ are stitched on the back.)
4. Flip over with the pocket facing down.
5. Pin the hook side of the Velcro™ to the top short edge opposite the folded pocket.
6. Stitch around all sides of the Velcro™.
7. Unpin the pocket so the placemat is flat. Leave pins to mark the top of the pocket. Pin the second piece of Velcro™ on the back. Put it

slightly below where the top of the pocket will be. This will ensure that the pocket will conceal the stitching.

8. Stitch Velcro™ strip all around the edges.

9. Turn over. Flip the pocket back in place.

10. Pin sides, stitch, and press.

11. Place around the armrest.

12. Repeat with the 2nd napkin for the other arm.

Use the "Wheel Chair Seatcover" made with a napkin as part of the ensemble.

Sailboat Fabric Variation Side Arm Bag

Decorative and directional designs such as this one create serious challenges, requiring extra manipulation to make sure the boats don't end up upside-down. Orient the napkins first to decide how the designs should run. The extra work is well worth the effort.

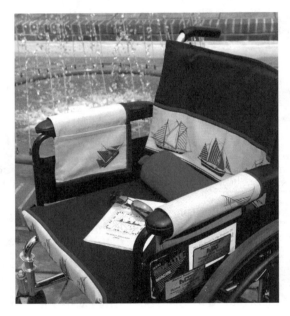

MATERIALS & NOTIONS

Thread
2 Napkins
Two 8-inch pieces of hook & loop Velcro™

---

1. Cut napkin in half.

2. Hem the cut side of one piece.

3. Using the other half, fold it to determine where the design should be so that the design will be on the front of the pocket. (This might require trimming of sides.)

4. Turn that piece WST and stitch up the cut side to form a pocket panel.

5. Turn RSO. Press.

6. Position the pocket on right side of the other section. Place pins to determine where to sew Velcro™. Stitches are hidden within the pocket.

7. Pin the hook side of the Velcro™ to the top short edge opposite the folded pocket. Stitch around all sides of the Velcro™.

8. Pin the second piece of Velcro™ on the back. Put slightly below where the top of the pocket would be. This will ensure that the pocket will conceal the stitching.

9. Place the pocket on the front so that the bottom edges align. Pin and stitch along the sides and bottom.

10. Attach the Velcro™ so that it will wrap around the armrest.

11. Repeat all steps for a second side arm bag.

NOTE: To make the **Seat Cover** *follow the pattern that uses one napkin for the cover. Make the* **Back Seat Cover** *using the pattern for the Patriotic Seat Cover. Follow the Rolled Pillow Pattern to make the* **pillow**.

My Notes

Scooter Cover-up

This cover is a terrific way to enhance the looks of a wonderfully liberating vehicle. In practically no time, a spiffy cover will be ready for that next trip out and about. Hey, wanna race?

Scooter Bag

MATERIALS & NOTIONS

Thread
1 Large solid woven texture kitchen towel
2 Dog collars (neck size 8-14 inches)

---

1. Fold towel horizontally RST so it is long and skinny.

2. Fold in half again to make equal fourths. Press along the folded edge.

3. Fold open leaving one side folded.

4. Stitch along the fold line.

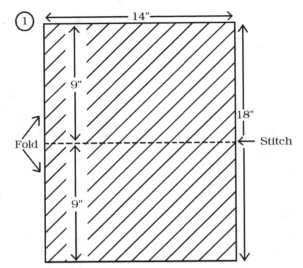

This next step is a little tricky, so read carefully!

5. Taking the two top corners, flip them back to the other two corners. The seam is now INSIDE and you have a finished side.

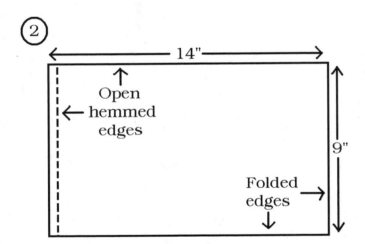

6. The other side is open with hemmed edges.

7. Press, pin the open side, and stitch.

8. If you don't want a bulky seam, you can trim off the hemmed edges at this point.

9. Turn so stitched seam is inside.

10. Press and top stitch along each side. This will encase the trimmed

seam so it won't unravel. (You now have three pockets.)

11. Cut the dog collars using the directions in the section on *Handles/ Hangers*.

12. The bag has four layers. Sandwich the cut ends of the dog collars between layer 1 and 2, and then in between layer 3 and 4 on top corner. Pin handles/hangers in place.

13. Stitch.

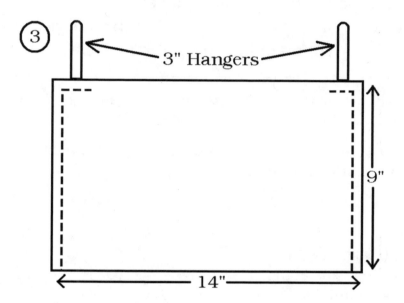

Scooter Back Cover

MATERIALS & NOTIONS

Thread
1 decorative kitchen towel
Two 3-inch pieces of hook & loop Velcro™
Optional – two 12-inch pieces of ribbon trim
One 18-inch piece of 1- or 2-inch wide ribbon
Optional: iron-on stitching tape

1. Fold the towel in half horizontally. Fold again horizontally. Mark the folds with pins. Unfold and lay flat.

Use either Velcro™ strips or ribbons. If using ribbon, turn under the raw edges before stitching in place.

2. You will have 2 pins on each side at the 1/4th mark. Pin ½ inch of loop piece on the wrong side at the top 1/4th pins. The longer portion will be hanging over the edge. Repeat on opposite side.

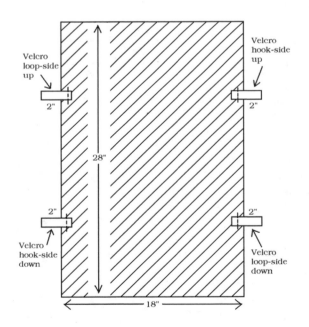

50

3.	Repeat this process with the hook pieces of Velcro™ on the wrong side at the 2 lower 1/4th pins.

4.	Stitch Velcro™ or ribbon.

5.	Place trim along the lower edge of the seat back to determine placement. Placing masking tape along a straight edge will ensure that the ribbon is sewn in a straight line.

6.	Pin the ribbon in place along the edge of the masking tape. Turn the raw edges of ribbon under on the ends. Topstitch along both sides of the ribbon, or use iron on tape.

7.	Place the cover on the back of the scooter. Attach Velcro™ strips on the sides or tie the ribbons.

Scooter Seat Cover

MATERIALS & NOTIONS

Thread
1 Smooth Kitchen Towel
Two 6-inch pieces of hook & loop Velcro™
One 9-inch strip of 1-inch wide elastic

1.	Measure the short end of the towel. Place pins 5 inches from each corner.

2.	Measure 10 inches down from the corners both sides. Place a pin for marking.

3.	Lay flat with the wrong side facing up. Place a ruler so that it touches the two pins on one side. Fold the corner triangle of fabric toward the center. Press along the fold. Repeat on the other side.

4.   Place on the seat to determine if it fits properly inside the back opening of the seat.

5.   Cut along the fold. Turn under twice. Pin.

6.   Press again and topstitch.

7.   Pin the loop pieces of Velcro™ on the WS top corners, and stitch in place. (See illustration.)

8.   Pin the hook pieces of Velcro™on the WS of the lower corners and stitch in place.

NOTE: Stitching on the elastic will make the cover fit better in the front. You might also want to sew Velcro™ strips onto the sides to hold the cover in place more securely.

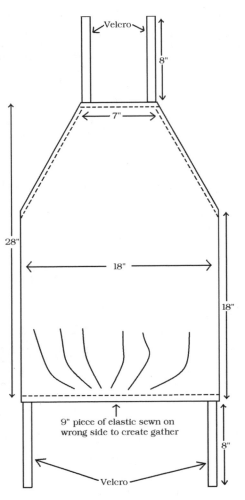

9.   Stretch elastic to determine its full length.

10. With elastic stretched, pin 1 inch in from the sides along the front edge.

11. As you stretch the elastic, sew along it in order to gather the front edge.

12. Place on the seat. Attach the Velcro strips underneath the seat for a snug fit.

Bags & Pockets

What's in a Name?

Each of the bags throughout this book is named for a special town in the lives of my family – it seemed fitting, since North Carolina is truly in my blood.

PATETOWN – My Lancaster, Pate, and Sasser families have lived in this small farming community in Wayne County since the mid-1700's. My mother's maiden name is Pate. My mother and father grew up about a half mile from each other – Daddy drove the school bus and Mama was the proctor on the bus. They married soon after Pearl Harbor. A few months later he went off to serve in the Army, ultimately surviving D-Day +1. In the meantime, my brother Martin was born in Mama's parents' home in Patetown. Upon Daddy's return, they settled into a life of farming, selling fertilizer, and working on the tobacco market. My sister Nan and I joined our brother in 1947 and 1953 respectively to make up our family.

GOLDSBORO – Goldsboro is a five-mile drive from Patetown. We made the trip almost daily. It was where we did all of our shopping, going to movies, banking, and going out to eat. We would say we were going "uptown" even though we drove down a country road to get there. It was always a treat to go to Herman Park to swing and ride the miniature train.

PIKEVILLE – Pikeville is located five miles north of Patetown. We used to know just about everyone who lived there. My parents and my siblings and I went to elementary and high school in Pikeville. We loved parties at the Scout Hut, fountain Coke at the drug store, and hamburgers at Buck's. I even got to do my student teaching in Kindergarten at Pikeville Elementary School under my mother's friend, Katherine Smith.

MOREHEAD CITY – My husband, William, and his family lived in Morehead City for almost 20 years. It is right across the sound from Atlantic Beach.

BOGUE SOUND – My Pate grandparents, Guy and Nora, bought a beach house in 1961 at Atlantic Beach on Bogue Sound. We still love going there with all of our children and Mama's two new great-grandchildren (who are now the fifth generation of our family to vacation there). My husband and I began our courtship on the "Circle" in Atlantic Beach.

ATLANTIC – This small fishing village is where my mother-in-law, Avis Styron Gorges, grew up. She could trace her families' roots in the area to the mid-1700's.

The Gorges Family lived there until 1961 and then moved to Morehead City. We now have a vacation home on land owned by the Stryon clan for many generations.

WILMINGTON – Driving about two hours south of Patetown on Highway 117 will land you in the growing port town of Wilmington. As young children, we always drove through Wilmington on our way to Carolina Beach. My husband, William, graduated from UNC-Wilmington, as did my nephew, Jonathan. William and I first met while he was a student there. Our son, Mark, is now a student at UNC-W.

CHAPEL HILL – My first trip to Chapel Hill was to take my brother, Martin, to college. Martin graduated from the University of North Carolina as did my sister-in-law Alice; my nieces, Megan, Ashley, and Mary; and just this past spring my son Chris.

RALEIGH – The capital of North Carolina is a one-hour drive west of Patetown. When we were children, Mama would take us shopping at Cameron Village and out for lunch at the K&W Cafeteria. We drove to Raleigh to see The Sound of Music on a huge movie screen – our first big city experience as children! I attended and graduated from Peace College, right in the heart of Raleigh. My brother-in-law, Jim Davis, graduated from North Carolina State University.

CARY – This one-time sleepy little town is just west of Raleigh. My sister, Nan, and her husband, Jim, moved there while I was a student at Peace College and Jim was at NCSU. Little did we know that most of our family would end up there years later. My sister's family, my brother's family, and my mother now all live in Cary. Mama lives at Glenaire Retirement Community.

GREENVILLE – About an hour northeast of Patetown is Greenville, the home of East Carolina University. Our grandmother, Mary (Molly) Williams Lancaster, was one of the school's first graduates when it was East Carolina Teacher's College. My sister Nan and I graduated from ECU with teaching degrees, and my nephew Staton recently graduated with a degree in art.

WILSON – Tobacco is Wilson's claim to fame. Daddy and Mama spent many years working at the tobacco auctions there. The smell of the cured tobacco and the sing-song of the auctioneer's voice was intoxicating to me as a child. In my adult years, I moved to Wilson to work for the NC Arts Council and later the Wilson Greene Mental Health Center. During that time I dated the man who would later become my husband.

NEW BERN – In order to get from Patetown to our family vacation home in Atlantic Beach, we had to drive through New Bern. Driving over the bridge downtown and looking at the wide expanse of the Neuse River was something we always looked forward to. Little did I know that this pretty town would one day become home to my family and the birthplace of two of my children. We moved here in 1986. Mama moved here in 1994 to live in an assisted living facility where she stayed for over six years before moving to Cary.

The Atlantic Bag

This bag is so easy and inexpensive to make you might want to get together a group of friends, coworkers, or church members for a few hours of sewing. In a short period of time, you could sew lots of these. A few days later plan an outing to a nursing home to distribute your handi-work. Expect to be welcomed with open arms!

MATERIALS & NOTIONS

Thread
1 Woven Placemat or any easily foldable Placemat
Two 8-inch pieces of 1-inch wide Ribbon
or
Two 4-inch pieces of hook & loop Velcro™

---

1. Fold one placemat into one thirds with the top flap approximately 2 inches shorter than the other two thirds. Press. (See illustration #1.)

2. Flip back the front flap. Pin the sides of the other two sections and stitch.

3. Cut the ribbon into two 18-inch pieces and fold each in half.

4. Lay the bag on a table with the front side down and the front flap up. Pin one ribbon to each of the two upper corners on the back side of the bag. (See illustration #2.

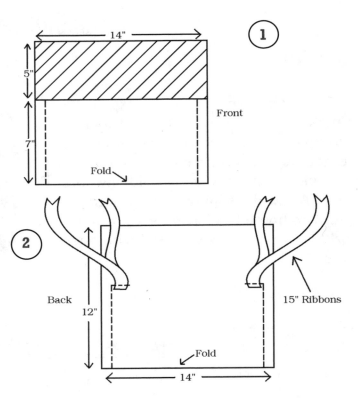

5. Variation: If using Velcro™ to attach the bag, cut two 4-inch pieces of Velcro. Sew on the top corners on the back with the front flap folded up.

6. Attach the bag to a walker, scooter handlebars, or the backrest bar of a seated walker.

Optional Pocket: A heavy-duty sandwich bag is perfect pocket for a bag that will not see lots of use. An often-used bag will require a sturdier pocket like a ready-made make up bag. Place the bag/baggie inside the envelope bag near the top fold. Stitch along the upper edge to hold in place.

The New Bern Bag

My friends Linda and Tom inspired this bag. Both said that all of the bags for wheelchairs were designed for the backs of the chairs. They wanted something that would fit on the side. The one I made for Tom worked great until he went out in the rain with it. Unless you make it out of vinyl, don't go out in the rain with this!

Another possibility for this bag is to attach it onto the side rail of a walker. Read carefully to determine the two different ways to attach the bag to different walkers and wheelchairs. You can make this bag using a dish towel or a placemat. With so many options, let your creativity take over.

MATERIALS & NOTIONS

(Walker Version)

1 terry cloth or plain cotton dish towel with same pattern on both sides – approximately 26" X 22"

Two 8-inch pieces of Snag Free Velcro™

Two 8-inch pieces of eyelet trim

Two 8-1/2-inch pieces of ½ inch wide ribbon

Two 8-inch pieces of pearl bead trim

Fabric Glue

Thread

1. Fold in half vertically WST. Press along fold. (See illustration #1.)
2. Open and lay flat right side up.
3. Fold under raw ends of ribbon and eyelet so trim is now the width of the shortest side.
4. Unfold towel. Lay it RSO. Using the fold lines as guides, find the upper right short edge. Pin trim.
5. Flip the towel over so you can pin other piece of trim to the opposite hemmed end of the towel.

Note: One trim will be on the right side of the towel and one trim will be on the wrong side of the towel. This is why the front and back of the fabric should look the same.

6. Stitch or glue on trim.
7. Fold in half horizontally. Press fold.
8. Fold again horizontally. Press fold.
9. Place pins in the folds along both edges.
10. Fold flat with wrong side up.
11. Use the folds as guidelines for the Velcro™. (See illustration #2.)
12. Pin the 2 pieces of Velcro™ on the ½ fold horizontal line 1 inch in from the sides.

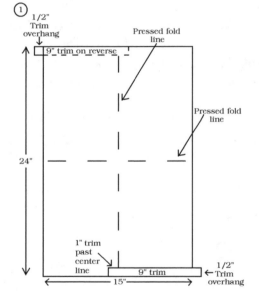

13. Stitch in place.
14. Cut two 2-inch pieces of ribbon or woven tape. Fold over straight side of D-ring. Pin raw edges.

15. Pin raw edges to the towel along the ¼ fold line below the Velcro™ strips.

16. Fold towel in half WST.

17. Pin and stitch the open side opposite the folded side.

18. Fold the trim edge up 4 inches to form a pocket. Pin and stitch on both sides. (See illustration #3.)

19. Fold up an 8-inch pocket on the opposite end. Pin along the lower edges. Turn down a 2-inch cuff.

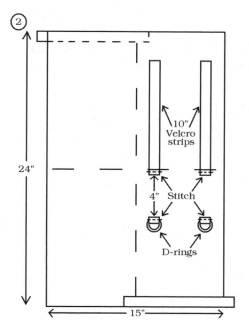

20. Pin sides of pocket. Stitch. (A zigzag stitch works well here for a little extra stability.)

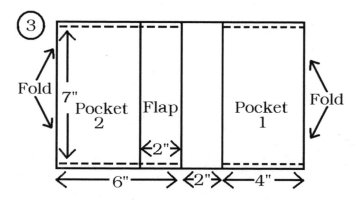

21. Place pieces of wax paper inside of the pockets so that when applying glue to the trim the pockets will not stitch together.

22. Glue the eyelet trim to the under edge of the fold down cuff. Turn under the ends of the eyelet. Repeat on the second pocket.

23. Glue the ribbon on top of the pocket cuff edges. Turn under the raw edges on the ends. Repeat on the second pocket.

24. Glue the tiny string beads along the top of the ribbons.

Placemat Version for Walker or Wheelchair

The placemat version of this bag is smaller. The turned up pockets will be 3 or 4 inches deep, rather than that of the larger 7-inch pocket and the 4-inch pocket.

On the back place only one ring and one strip of one-sided hook and loop-type Velcro™ since it will be smaller. The bag can also be attached by placing Velcro™ strips horizontally where the Velcro™ strips and the D-rings are marked on the illustration.

My Notes

_____

_____

_____

_____

_____

_____

_____

_____

_____

_____

_____

_____

_____

_____

_____

_____

_____

_____

The Morehead Pocket

I was given an eyeglasses case made from a potholder at an Extension Homemakers Club meeting. I immediately thought that this would be a great idea to modify and adapt for use with mobility items. (With the corner flipped down it is easier to retrieve items inside.)

These groups do a great deal for the community. Mama was a charter member of the Stoney Creek Extension Homemakers Club in Wayne County, NC, and a 4-H Leader for my brother and sister.

Minimal sewing is required for this holder, so 4-H Clubs would love making several for a community project. Hang it on the tubular part of a wheelchair or walker using a decorative shower curtain hook or a piece of two-sided Velcro™.

MATERIALS & NOTIONS

1 Potholder with a loop
1 Large button
Decorative shower curtain hanger or Velcro™

---

1. Fold potholder in half so that the loop is on the top corner. Press.

2. Fold the right-hand top corner down to the left at an angle (aligning the front top edge with the left edge). Pin.

3. Place button on the turned down flap and stitch in place securely. This turned-down flap makes it much more accessible to the items in it.

4. Pin along bottom and up the side to the point of the flap. Stitch.

5. Hang on walker or handle bars of scooter with hanger or Velcro.

The Greenville Pocket

This bag can be described in three words: Easy, easy, easy! There is no sewing involved unless you want to sew on a bit of trim. Little ones will love helping to make a bag for a grandparent or friend. It is extra roomy for a telephone, remote control, or even a small paperback book.

NOTE: If a child is helping, be especially careful with the HOT iron!

MATERIALS & NOTIONS

1 Hot mitt
Decorative Iron-on transfers
Trim
Iron-on tape
Wax paper
Decorative shower curtain hanger or One-Wrap Velcro™

---

1. Put a piece of wax paper inside the mitt so that the transfers and trim don't adhere to both sides.

2. Position the trim and appliqué/transfers onto mitt.

3. Following directions for iron-on tape, iron trim and transfers onto mitt.

4, Hang on walker or handle bars of scooter with curtain hanger or Velcro.

The Cary Bag

This little bag will please any recipient because it will fit on all mobility devices. No measuring required and very little sewing is necessary. Hot pads feature such cute special interest designs. Get ready for lots of smiles when presenting this cute little bag to a loved one.

MATERIALS & NOTIONS

One Wrap Velcro™ – long enough to wrap around a wheelchair arm or metal bars of a walker, or
2 Adjustable dog collars (neck size 8-14 inches)
2 Hot pads (best if the loops are on the top corners)

NOTE: *If you find pads that you love with loops on the center top, just turn one loop inside and stitch it so that it isn't visible, or turn loop(s) under and sew plastic rings to the corners (see photo).*

1. Position the two hot pads WST.
2. Pin along the sides and along the bottom
3. Stitch on the sides and bottom.
4. Place the two dog collars through the two loops and hang on the handle bars. This is a no-sew hanger.

The Chapel Hill Bag

The bag is inexpensive and extremely functional. Folks will love using it on their scooter handle bars, electric wheelchair arms, walkers or the backrest rail of a Rollator™. The use of holiday napkins, brightly colored napkins, or even a hunting print bandana can turn it into a true eye-catcher.

When finished, it has an opening in the center that is a perfect place for a rolled up magazine or newspaper. On top of that, it even has two pockets for a remote control, book, or keys.

Make sure you try one with a photo pocket to show off relatives or vacation spots! Try tucking in a newspaper or magazine to show one of its best features when giving it as a gift.

MATERIALS & NOTIONS

Thread
1 Cloth napkin
Two 1-inch D-rings
Two 9-inch pieces of Snag-Free Velcro™

NOTE: See Photo Pocket Section for further instructions.

1.   Fold napkin into four sections. Press to form guidelines.

NOTE: If putting on the photo pocket, do it at this time. Center the pocket on the middle of the upper right-hand corner, and follow Photo Pocket directions.

2. Loop 1 inch of the 9-inch Velcro™ strip over the straight side of the D-ring with the hook sides touching. Baste in place with a large stitch.

3. Pin the D-ring and Velcro™ 1 inch in from the corners on the right side of the bottom right hand corner.

4. The hook-side of the Velcro™ will be facing down on the right side of the napkin.

5. Fold in half lengthwise with the photo pocket (optional) and the Velcro/D-rings facing up.

6. Pin the hemmed edge and stitch.

7. Fold in half with the open ends touching. Press.

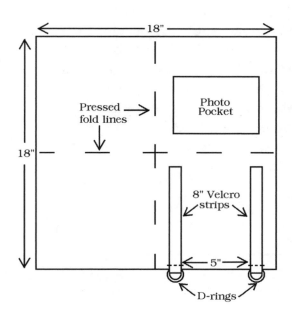

8. Stitch along the pressed fold. (This will give a bottom to the pockets on either side.)

9. Place on the bar of a walker, scooter handle bars, side armrest or seated walker backrest bar

The Wilmington Bag

The bag is incredibly stylish. It will look especially great on the seated walker backrest bar! My teenage daughter and her friends liked this bag so much that I even made one for her using purse-type handles. Make one for a friend to go with her favorite "Sunday Best Outfit".

MATERIALS & NOTIONS

Thread
1 Quilted placemat
1 Cloth napkin
One 36-inch piece of 1-inch wide ribbon
Rickrack or upholstery trim
2 colorful buttons
Optional closures – magnetic closure or Velcro™ tabs

---

1. Fold placemat in half horizontally. Pin sides. Stitch sides.
2. Turn RSO and turn the upper edge down 2 to 3 inches to get a visual idea of how the bag will appear when finished. (For a taller/ larger bag, don't turn down the edge.)

NOTE: If you want to add trim to the top edge, this is the time to do it. Pin the trim in place along the edge. Topstitch in place.

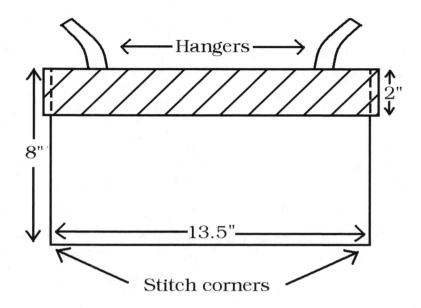

3. Make the bottom bag corner by pinching flat the side seam so that it touches the bottom seam. Pin 2 to 3 inches up from the point. Stitch across.

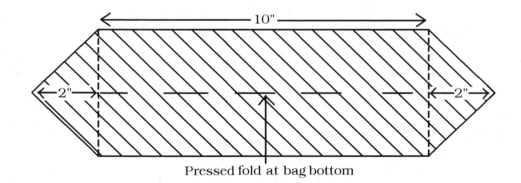

Pressed fold at bag bottom

Bag Bottom

1. Cut out a piece of plastic 8 or 9 inches by 3 inches. Needle punch plastic with the little holes is perfect.

2. Using a napkin cut a piece 9 inches X 3 inches. Fold it in half-lengthwise RST. Stitch across the raw edge end, and up the long side.

3.   Turn RSO. Press.

4.   Slide plastic into the pocket.

5.   Place the finished pocket in the bottom of the bag and stitch in the corners to hold into place.

Handle Options

Go to the *Handles/Holder* Section to decide which style you prefer. Dog collars and Velcro™ work best.

1.   Position the handles along the upper portion of the folded-down edge. Or pin on the edge if a taller/larger bag is desired.)

2.   Place handles about 2 to 3 inches from the side seam.

3.   Pin 4 Velcro™ pieces inside. Position so that the hook and loop strips will attach to each other when wrapped over a bar. Pin so that the stitches that hold the Velcro™ in place will not be visible when the edge is turned down.

4.   Turn the edge up.

5.   Stitch the 4 Velcro ™ pieces in a square to provide stability.

6.   Fold down the edge.

7.   Optional: For decoration, stitch a button on top of the folded edge and the Velcro™.

8.   Hang on a walker side or front bar, scooter handles, or backrest bar of a seated walker.

CLOSURE OPTIONS

• Velcro™ square or circle

• Magnetic clasp

• Button with a loop.

The Wilson Bag

Interesting trim makes this bag a big-time winner. The sewing takes only a few minutes. Depending on the trim and the placemat, it can be sophisticated or whimsical. What a super little bag for a wallet, cell phone, iPod®, headphones, or other small items.

Since the Velcro™ can be adjusted to the arm circumference the bag is perfect for department store and other types of wheelchairs. With short hangers, it can be used on walkers as well.

MATERIALS & NOTIONS

Thread
1 placemat
Two 12-inch strips of two-sided Velcro
Approximately 7 inches of trim of choice
(Ribbon, pompoms, elastic hair bobbles, etc.)

NOTE: If you want to use loop and ball ponytail holders as fringe, pin the metal clasps so that they will be sandwiched in between the finished front edge. Apply rickrack or ribbon on top of the edge.

1. Fold the placemat in half-lengthwise RST. Press along fold.
2. Unfold. Place flat facing *right side up*. Pin, tape, or baste the trim along one side of the upper right side edge of the short end.
3. Pin the fringe/hair bobbles, etc. on the backside of the top edge. (Later it will be sandwiched in place between two layers of the place

mat edge.) The fringe/dangle part will hang off the fabric edge. The rickrack will be on the opposite side of the placemat fabric.

4. Baste fringe.
5. Fold place mat in half along the fold RST. Pin long side edge.
6. Stitch long side and turn RSO. Press.
7. Topstitch across trim. This will "sandwich" the dangling trim.
8. Fold the untrimmed short edge up approximately 7 inches to form a pocket. Pin sides.
9. Topstitch on both sides of pocket. This forms two pockets.
10. Fold Velcro™ in half to determine the centerline. Pin to mark center.
11. Pin the center of the Velcro™ strip to the upper back edge of the top flap.
12. Open flap. Zigzag stitch Velcro™ in place.

NOTE: *If you want to use Velcro™ in a coordinating color, you might need to use the standard type with hook on one side and loop on the other. Place one inch of each of the ends of the hook and loop so that they attach. Now sew that 1 inch attached portion to the top back of the bag. Repeat on the other side. Wrap around the arm or handle bars and attach.*

The Patetown Bag

The idea of creating a sewing pattern book began after I made this bag for my mother in 2001 around Christmas. When I gave it to her, she immediately exclaimed, "Pretty!" It was the closest thing to a functional and colorful new purse or pocket-book that Mama had received in years!

This little bag can prove to be a great lift to their every day life. Make sure you take it over the edge with creativity. Make it fun, colorful, and fitting to the personality of the recipient.

<u>MATERIALS & NOTIONS</u>

Thread
2 Decorative placemats
or
1 Decorative placemat & one plain placemat
One 36-inch long piece of 1-inch wide ribbon

---

1. Position placemats WST.
2. Pin sides and bottom. Stitch.

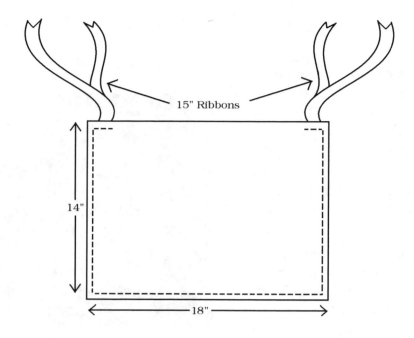

15" Ribbons

14"

18"

3. Cut ribbon so that you have two 18-inch pieces.

4. Fold each piece of ribbon in half.

5. Sandwich the folded ribbon inside the placemat corners at a slight angle outward on each side (loose ends out). Pin.

6. Stitch back and forth several times to add strength.

Brimmed Cap

This is one of three easy ways to add a personal touch to your bag! Two more variations follow.

Let this bag be a billboard for a favorite team or sport. Men love to get a little friendly competition going!

MATERIALS & NOTIONS

2 Placemats

1 "special" cap

2 One-Wrap Velcro™ Strips (hangers) or

36 inches of 1-inch wide ribbon

---

1. Fold the back of a brimmed hat into the front so that it will flatten.

2. Fold the placemat in half to determine the center front.

3. Using masking tape or pins, mark the centerline and the ¼ line on each side of the center.

4. Position the hat on the placemat, pin it at the top and along the sides.

5. Backstitch (solid back and forth zigzag) at the center top. Repeat at two or three places on each side. Proceed according to instructions for the *Patetown Bag*.

Bag With Marine Patches

My husband, Will, was a big help when it came to personalizing bags for men. He suggested that I go to a military surplus store. Go to one in your area for lots of great ideas!

MATERIALS & NOTIONS

2 Placemats
Thread
Decorative sew on patches
12-inch piece of hook & loop Velcro™
40 inches twill trim (1-inch wide)
Fabric Glue

---

1. Lay patches on placemat to determine where they look best.
2. Apply "iron on type glue" to the back of the patches.
3. Iron the patches in place.
4. Stitch or glue additional trim in place on top and bottom edges.
5. Follow instructions for the *Patetown Bag* to complete.
6. Refer to the *Handle/Hanger* section to make hook and loop Velcro™ hangers.

License Plate Bag

Travelers can bring back a license plate as a souvenir of a special trip or get a license plate to proclaim a special alliance to a team, state or any other special interest. In order to change the plates for a little variety, make removable hangers.

My husband, Will, came up with this idea. Being a car enthusiast in every way, he knew that other men would like having a vanity plate on a vehicle with or without a motor.

MATERIALS & NOTIONS

2 Placemats
2 Cable Ties
Ribbon or trim of choice
(length of top & bottom of placemats)
2 D-rings
Two 2-inch pieces of Snag Free Velcro™

---

1. Select ribbon to trim top and bottom edges to frame plate.

2. Using the same ribbon, cut two 4-inch pieces of ribbon and loop them around a 1- to 2-inch D-ring.

3. Glue or stitch ribbon in place near the top of the placemat. Align with holes in license plate.

4. Pin ribbon or trim along the top edge, covering the raw edges of the loop ribbons. Stitch.

5. Stitch trim or ribbon along the bottom edge.

6. Thread the two 2-inch Snag Free Velcro™ strips through the holes in the top of the license plate. Using the strips attach the license plate to the "D" rings hanging on the ribbons.

7. Fold cable tie in half. Sandwich folded middle into the upper corner. Pin. Stitch securely. Repeat on the other side.

My Notes

The Goldsboro Bag

I just love this pattern! Due to its versatility, I find myself using it for many different people. It is almost identical to the Patetown Bag. The only difference is that you use only one placemat to make it. The smaller size of the bag works well with Rollators™, scooters and walkers.

Like the Patetown Bag, this is a perfect bag to utilize linens that highlight an individual's special interests. It can also be a fun and interesting-looking bag if you make it out of wild jazzy patterns. Using metallic or sequined placemats can even create a classy evening bag. This bag is very versatile and the variations are unlimited!

Materials & Notions

1 placemat

Thread

36 inches of 1-inch wide ribbon or

Follow directions for alternate Handles/Hangers

Follow the instructions for the *Patetown Bag*.

Fur Trim & Monogram Variation

Fur Trim bag made by Peggy Monterio

Here is a bag that demonstrates how versatile this pattern can be. It can be rather rowdy with a fake fur trim or preppy and cute with ribbons and bows!

1. Fold placemat in half to determine where to place monogram. Press along the fold.

2. Stitch on monogram. If you don't own a machine with this feature take the placemat to a local store that specializes in embroidery. Consider asking a friend. (I asked my friend, Peggy, to monogram a bag and she did a super job!)

3. Fold again and measure the shortest side.

4. Measure the length of the shortest side of the placemat and multiply by two. Add 1 inch for the seam allowance. Using that measurement cut a strip of fake fur 4 inches wide.

5. Topstitch or hem by hand one long edge of the fur.

6. Fold the fur in half so that there is a 3-inch centerfold. Cut along the fold. These will be the trim for the front and back top edges of the bag.

7. Place the right side of the fur facing the wrong side of the placemat. Pin the raw edge of the fur to the top edge of the placemat. Repeat on the other top edge.

8. Stitch.

9. Pin sides and edges of the fur trim turned up. Stitch.

10. When stitching on hangers keep the fur trim turned up in order to hide the stitches underneath the trim.

11. Go to *Handles/Hangers* for instructions for sewing "looped ribbon hangers". The hangers shown in the photo have wide rick rack sewn on the ribbon for a decorative touch.

My Notes

_____

_____

_____

_____

_____

_____

_____

_____

_____

_____

_____

_____

_____

_____

_____

_____

_____

_____

_____

Once You've Finished Your Bag...

Here are a few thoughtful items to tuck inside if the bag is a gift. Give special consideration to the needs, limitations, and interests of the recipient!

- Tissues
- Small photo album
- Paperback book
- Magazines
- Hand wipes
- Small bottle of lotion
- Candy
- Small tape or CD player
- CDs or tapes
- Magnifying glass
- Box of checkers and a board
- Pen and notepad
- Binoculars
- Manicure set
- Playing cards
- Devotional book

Add a decorative luggage tag to the bag for identification purposes. This will ensure that the walker or wheelchair stays with its owner. A laminated business or gift card works well as a tag.

Decorate a Cane

This isn't a sewing project and it definitely doesn't use linens in the materials list. However, this idea seemed very fitting for this book because it is a terrific way to enhance a very popular mobility aid – the walking cane.

A couple of years ago my friend, Barbara Holderby, had an incredibly clever idea. Her mother insisted that she didn't need a cane for walking but Barbara felt that she did. To tackle this problem, Barbara took a very creative approach. Being a tole painter, she took out her paints and created a wooden cane with a trailing ivy vine. Along the vine, she wrote the names of all of her mother's grandchildren. She said that her mother immediately began to use the cane, constantly showing it to her friends and telling them all about her grandchildren. I still love the mental picture of her mother showing off her lovely cane!

I confess that I am not much of a painter but I do love to tear paper and glue things to items so I decided to turn to decoupage. Back in high school and college, my friends and I had a great time covering empty pretty wine bottles with images and words from magazines. Maybe you could get your teenagers involved in this project!

MATERIALS

Wooden or metal cane
Fine sandpaper
White glue or decoupage medium
Sponge brush
Damp rag
Wax paper
Clear acrylic spray or polyurethane
Rubber tip for canes or chair legs
Color copied family photos, catalogs, magazines, etc.
Photographs (I know I always have lots of "double prints" left over.)

NOTE: Color or black and white photo copies on thin paper work better than photos because thick photo paper won't smooth down well. If you do use photos, peel open the corner with your fingernails and tear off the back paper.

INSTRUCTIONS:

1. Lightly sand the cane and then wipe it off clean.

2. Decide if you want to use family photos, brightly colored tissue paper, photos from a magazine, flower catalogs, or tool catalogs for your cane collage.

3. Tear images into pieces that fit on the cane if wrapped around one time or that fit on the side of the cane. Tear images into small pieces featuring items or people's faces. *Torn edges blend better than cut edges.*

4. Try a few images on the cane before applying glue. Decide where you want to place each piece. Place the first image face-down on a sheet of wax paper on a counter.

5. Mix a tiny bit of water into your chosen decoupage medium, such as white glue, to make it easy to spread. Apply the medium onto the first image with a soft paint brush. Start with the tip of the crook of the cane and continue to layer them down the cane. Repeat with all images as you glue them on the cane.

   NOTE: Starting at this point and then layering down gives a better covering than just putting them on at random.

6. Using the paint brush, apply more of the glue mixture onto the top of the image. Keep layering the pieces down the cane. Use your fingers or a tiny roller brush to smooth the paper as you are applying it to the cane. (Don't worry about blank spaces – you can go back and add some smaller photos at the end.)

7. Allow to dry. Once dry, apply two more coats of glue/medium and let these coats dry between applications.

8. To make the finish more durable, apply a final coat of clear acrylic spray or polyurethane to the dry cane.

9. Put a rubber tip on the end of the cane.

Photo locations

Mitchell's Hardware - New Bern, NC
Tryon Palace Gardens - New Bern, NC
Fort Totten Park - New Bern, NC
Union Point Park - New Bern, NC
National Avenue - New Bern, NC
Fort Macon State Park – Atlantic Beach, NC
Charter Boat Docks – Morehead City, NC
Yvonne Gray and George Baka home – Merritt, NC
Courtyards at Berne Village – New Bern, NC

Order Information

To order additional copies of Walk & Roll *please contact:*

Lynn Lancaster Gorges
The Creative Caregiver
3910 Highway 70 East
New Bern, NC 28560

LynnGorges@creativecaregiver.com
www.creativecaregiver.com
www.thecreativecaregiver.com

You can also order individual sewing patterns for items to use for bathing, dining, resting, and decorating a nursing home room. Some of the patterns are listed below. Go to our web site for more information.

- Busy aprons and busy lap quilt
- Four aprons
- Bathing robe and apron
- Decorating a nursing home room with a Bed in a Bag
- Daily organizer for clothing

About the Author

Lynn Lancaster Gorges

Author Lynn Lancaster Gorges of New Bern, North Carolina, is the mother of three children, ages 15, 19 and 22. She and her husband, William, are the owners of Battleground Antiques, Inc., and Historic Textiles Studio.

Lynn has an Associate of Arts degree from Peace College and a Bachelor of Science in Education from East Carolina University. Lynn has worked as an elementary school teacher, an arts administrator for the North Carolina Arts Council, a consultant for an Employee Assistance Program, and a consultant for Cuisinarts. For the past fifteen years, Lynn has been a textile conservator. Additionally, Lynn has been extremely involved in volunteering in her children's schools, the First Presbyterian Church of New Bern, and various other community organizations. Her favorite hobbies include sewing, reading, and traveling. She and her family have recently completed their goal of visiting all fifty states.